Today...

Encouraging grieving children to express their inner feelings

Brittney N. Smith

Copyright © 2010 Brittney N. Smith

All rights reserved.

ISBN: 146114762X
ISBN-13: 978-1461147626

DEDICATION

This book is dedicated to all children who have a voice and feel their voice is not heard.
Always continue to live, love, write, and dream big! Through it all, know someone loves you!

BNS

About the book

Today was created for children whom lost a loved one during such an impressionable stage in their life. This book is to help children learn to acknowledge and understand their feelings of grief and pain. Everyday children lose a loved one, whether it be to death, incarceration, divorce, or separation . Children do not understand why their loved one was taken from them so abruptly, and what life will become afterwards. The purpose of this book is for a child to read this story of a grieving child, and be encouraged to use the provided journaling pages to positively express their inner feelings. These pages will become a keepsake and used at a later time for comfort and support by the child.

TABLE OF CONTENTS

Today ...	**6**
Writing Journal Pages	**18**
Drawing and Picture Journal Pages	**32**
Note from Author	**46**

I feel sad today, because someone I love is gone away.
So, I am very sad today.

I CRIED TODAY,
BECAUSE I THOUGHT
OF THEM WHEN I
WENT TO PLAY,
THEN I REMEMBERED
SOMEONE ONCE TOLD
ME, IT WILL BE OK.
BUT I STILL FEEL
LIKE CRYING TODAY.

Sometimes I sit quietly and think of their smile,
And how warm and cuddly their hugs were,
So, I wrap my arms around myself and squeeze real tight,
And then I smile.

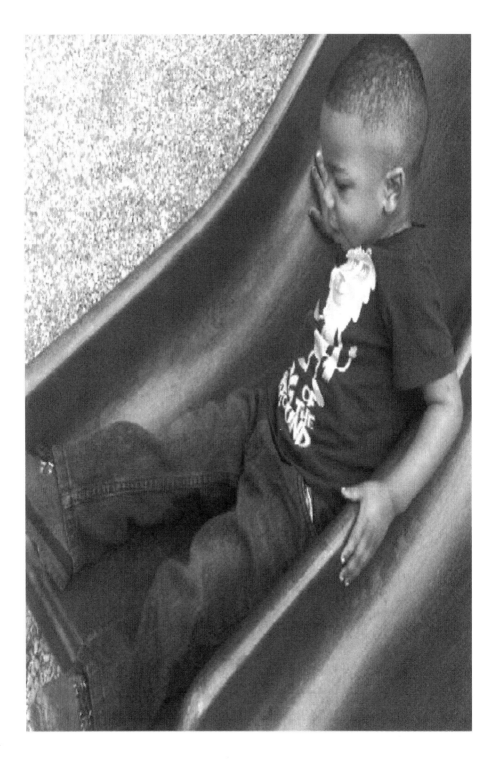

I remember how playing in the park was fun, when they caught me at the end of the slide, over and over because it was my favorite ride!

Those days were fun!

NOW I UNDERSTAND THAT IT'S OK IF SOMETIMES I AM FEELING SAD OR A BIT LONELY. THERE ARE ALSO TIMES WHEN I BELIEVE THERE IS NO ONE WHO CAN CONSOLE ME.

Even though I may not see my loved one again, I promise them this, When I start to feel a certain way, I will write, And tell them how I am feeling that day.

I will keep a journal in remembrance of them, and even though it hurts, I will always think about how much I love and miss them!

Instructions:

Please use the next twelve journal pages to write on days that you want to cry, scream, shout, laugh, or just let it all out! Always know you have the power to express yourself, and you can practice that in your own journal. Add pages as needed or start a new journal in a notebook. Whatever you do, please do not stop expressing yourself.

EXAMPLE ENTRY

Date: March 3, 2011

Today I feel... like running outside in the rain because it reminds me when my daddy and I would run in rain puddles. This makes me feel closer to him, even though I know he is gone away.

_____

_____

_____

_____

Date:_____

Today I feel...

_____

_____

_____

_____

_____

_____

_____

_____

_____

_____

_____

Date:_____

Today I feel...

Date:_____

Today I feel...

_____

_____

_____

_____

_____

_____

_____

_____

_____

_____

_____

_____

Date:_____

Today I feel...

Date:_____

Today I feel…

_____

_____

_____

_____

_____

_____

_____

_____

_____

_____

_____

Date:_____

Today I feel...

_____

_____

_____

_____

_____

_____

_____

_____

_____

_____

_____

Date:_____

Today I feel...

_____

_____

_____

_____

_____

_____

_____

_____

_____

_____

_____

Date:_____

Today I feel...

_____

_____

_____

_____

_____

_____

_____

_____

_____

_____

_____

Date:_____

Today I feel...

_____

_____

_____

_____

_____

_____

_____

_____

_____

_____

_____

Date:_____

Today I feel...

_____

_____

_____

_____

_____

_____

_____

_____

_____

_____

Date:_____

Today I feel…

Date:_____

Today I feel...

Instructions:

Please use the next twelve blank pages to draw or paste a picture of what is on your mind. You can do this anytime, but especially on the days when talking to others may not be an option. Draw happy faces, sad faces, pictures of you and your loved one, or paste your favorite picture! When these pages are filled, ask a grown-up to get you a new spiral notebook or grab some blank pieces of paper and continue drawing or pasting memories.

Keep your loved ones memory alive by sharing what you are feeling inside!

Example drawing
Date: March 3, 2011

Thinking of you makes me smile!

Date: _____

Date: _____

Date: _____

Date: _____

Date: _____

Date: _____

Date: _____

Date: _____

Date: _____

Date: _____

Date: _____

Look for future additions to this soon-to-be series of self-help books for children and other book projects.

Follow the author, Brittney Smith, on Facebook (BSmithPublications) or email her at bsmithpublications@gmail.com with any inquiries about this book or future publications.

Special Offer

Send them a smile!

Sweetz Boutique has a sweet spot for kids, therefore, we are offering a special "Today I Smile" cookie pack that can be sent to your special child of choice.

This is a great opportunity for school counselors, church members, or any caring individual to show a grieving child that someone is thinking of them.

For just $5.00 (plus s/h) send a child a

"Make them Smile" Cookie Pack

- 4 tasty homemade and decorated sugar cookies
- Individually wrapped
- Packaged and shipped as a gift to the child of your choice

Email: sweetzboutique@gmail.com
Phone: (210) 880-4901

Visit us online to take advantage of this offer:

http://www.sweetzboutique.com/#!__today-i-smile

Made in the USA
Columbia, SC
07 February 2022